HOW CRONY
CAPITALISM
CRUSHED THE
MIDDLE CLASS
AND KILLED
THE ECONOMY

How Crony Capitalism Crushed the Middle Class and Killed the Economy
Copyright © 2012 by David Gerson

ISBN: 978-0-9858835-0-8

All rights reserved. No part of this book may be reproduced or transmitted in any form or by any means without written permission from the author.

Dedication

To those whose shoulders I stand on; Kris Broberg, Michael Neitzel, Niklas Ludwig, Nick Caron, Sean Wright, Holly Hilden, Robert Gough, Jerry Hallenkamp, Leah Schimon, Eric Sayward, Mitch Rossow and Mark Johnson.

To my handlers who appreciate that I can't be managed, only suppressed; Chris Allen, Robin Young and Jim Hall.

To the following families; Heinstein, Fabian, Ausborn, Horn, Cabitt and Ganz.

Table of Contents

Preface 7

Income and Wealth in America 9

Postulate Key Points 14

Chapter 1: Trade Deficit Disorder 17

Chapter 2: Real Beasts of Debt Burden 25

Chapter 3: The Duke of Moral Hazard 33

Chapter 4: Private Sectored 41

Chapter 5: Trade Enemy Within 51

Chapter 6: Battle of the Wonks 59

Chapter 7: Disinheritance 71

Postscript: The Lights Are Off But Everybody's Home . 79

Preface

The perpetuation of economic myths to support political agendas has become endemic. We live in an increasingly complex globally-connected world where the truth is becoming easier to bury beneath poll-tested sound bites.

Many of us tend to cope with complexity by inventing simple adaptations to these myths that support our views and the way we wish to interpret the world. This tendency facilitates the transgressions of those in the position to manipulate and exploit whatever myths happen to be most lucrative for themselves and their privileged partners. But, it also awakens those of us whose political agenda is targeted on exposing these dangerous myths and working to end the transgressions. Doing so is what this book is all about.

Most politicians do not understand economics. And unfortunately, neither do most economists; who force all evidence through the lens of the strain of academic dogma from which they were fed and seek to validate to retain their perceived value.

Our greatest weapon against economic subjugation is to discover and disseminate the truth. This book attempts to expose the effects of crony capitalism through an explanation of the basic economics through which it manifests, and identify the key levers we should focus on pulling to shift the tide back toward an even playing field.

I hope this book will help to improve the conversation and that it will be further enhanced by the contributions of economic truth seekers wherever they may be found.

Income and Wealth in America

Percentage of Income Growth Captured by Top 1%

- Top 1% captured 93% of income growth, 2009-2010
- Top 1% captured 52% of income growth, 1993-2010

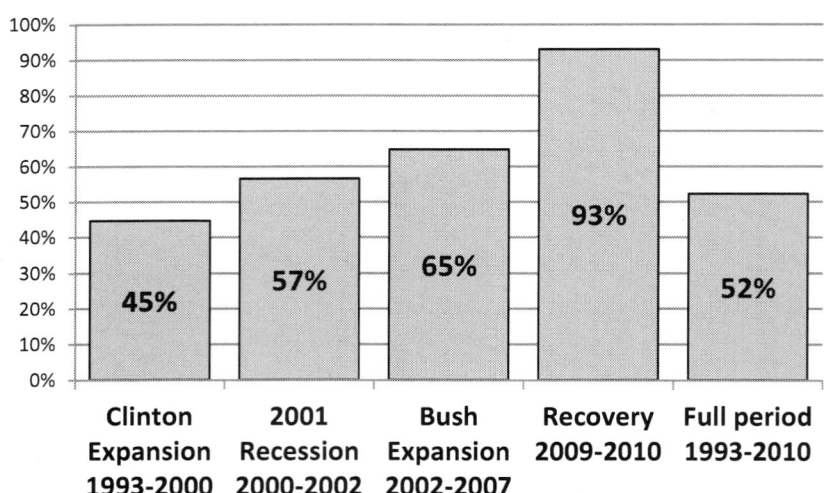

(Piketty-Saez)

Income Growth / Decline Between 1970 and 2010

- Income for the Top 1% increased by 119%
- Income for the Bottom 90% decreased by 23%

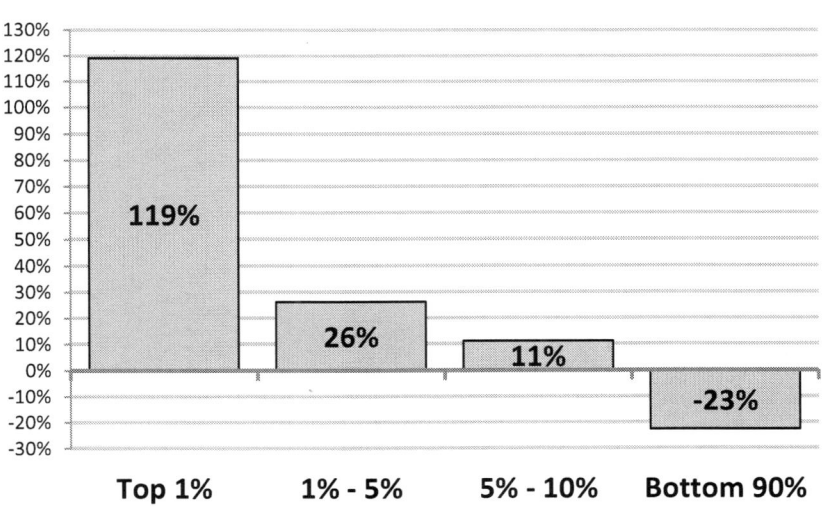

(Piketty-Saez)

Income Distribution in 2007

Top 1%:   24%
Top 5%:   39%
Top 10%:   50%
Top 20%:   61%
Bottom 80%: 39%

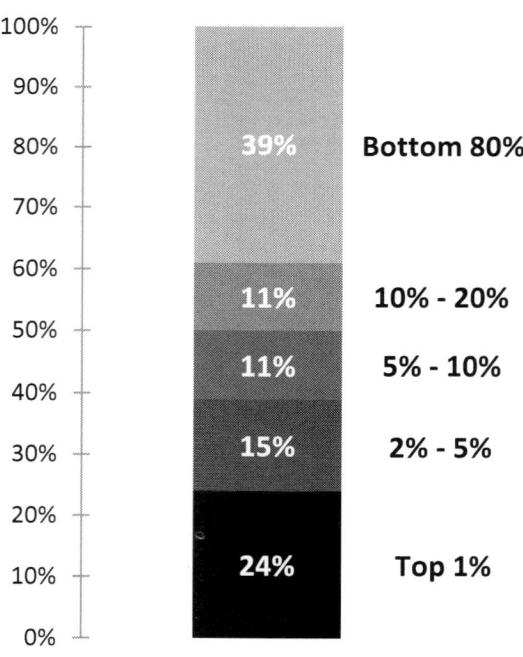

(G.William Domhoff, Picketty Saez)

Ownership of Financial Wealth in 2007

Top 1%:   43%
Top 5%:   72%
Top 10%:   83%
Top 20%:   93%
Bottom 80%   7%

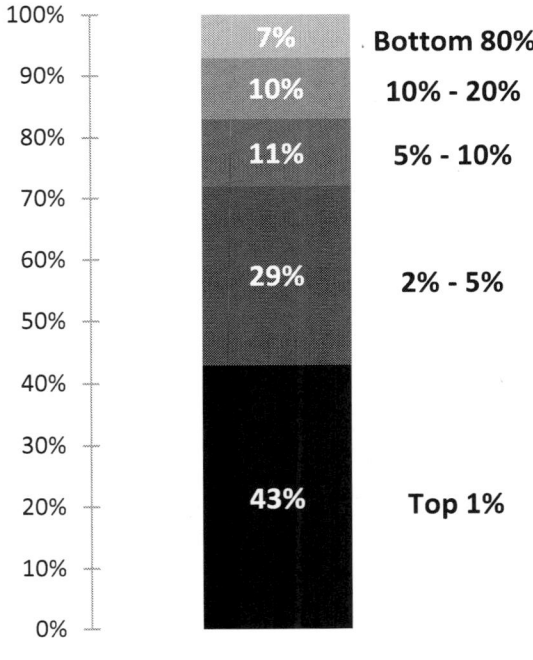

(G.William Domhoff)

Postulate Key Points

- America has an **Income Distribution Problem**
  - This manifests symptoms of an **Aggregate Demand Problem**

- We must now think of America having **Two Private Sectors**
  - The **Wealthy Minority** (which includes **Corporations**)
  - The **Non-Wealthy Majority** who have significantly impaired balance sheets (and have seen their standard of living decrease)

- **Crony Capitalism** creates distortions which benefit the wealthy
  - **Bigger Government** increases **Wealth Disparity**
  - **Crony Capitalism, Bigger Government** and **Wealth Disparity** comprise a self-reinforcing feedback loop

- **Fundamental Economic Principles:**
  - What we produce is equal to our income
  - A trade deficit creates a loss of income
  - If we save more than we earn the economy will decrease
  - If we deficit spend (from prior savings or by borrowing) more than we earn the economy will increase

- **Key Economic Dynamics:**
  - Our Income Distribution Problem is resulting in the Non-Wealthy no longer being able to deficit spend enough to make up for the desire of the increasingly Wealthy to save
  - The Wealthy who are saving include Americans, Foreigners and Corporations

- **The Federal Reserves Most Egregious Actions:**
  - Allowing the Federal Government to be fiscally irresponsible through supportive monetary policies
    - Allowing government to grow – reducing our productivity, global competitiveness and standard of living
  - Leading us into a long-term debt-deflation deleveraging scenario
  - Institutionalizing moral hazard and its resultant malinvestment

- **Stimulus and the Debt:**
  - Stimulus continues covertly in the form of budget deficits
  - The real burden of the debt:
    - Incentives: Increased debt increases marginal taxes on the productive workers and creates a disincentive to pursue productive activities
    - Distributions: Taxes to pay the interest on the debt is paid by those who must work to those who own the debt; transferring the ability to purchase goods and services from the productive citizens to the wealthy
    - Distortions: Debt allows bigger government which increases distortions (which benefit the lobbyist's special interest groups) and reduces our productivity and standard of living

- **China has been waging an economic war on the U.S.** which has undermined our economic security
  - Politicians have colluded the plunder to their crony's benefit

- **There are no Silver Bullets**
  - We must maximize our productivity to increase our standard of living
    - Removing government distortions to create efficient markets
    - Eliminating inefficiencies by minimizing government
  - We must become globally competitive and a net exporter

Chapter One

Trade Deficit Disorder

So you think you can tell,
Heaven from hell,
Blue skies from pain.
Can you tell a green field,
From a cold steel rail?
A smile from a veil?
Do you think you can tell?
Did they get you to trade,
Your heroes for ghosts?
Hot ashes for trees?
Hot air for a cool breeze?
Cold comfort for change?
Did you exchange,
A walk on part in a war,
For a lead role in a cage?

"Wish You Were Here" - Pink Floyd

When we run a trade deficit we are getting real goods and services in exchange for digital numbers in an importer's bank account, which represents dollars. Inflation erodes the value of those dollars so that they become an ever-smaller claim on our future goods and services. On the surface, this sounds advantageous: we are receiving real goods and services today from other countries that we can enjoy, which increases our standard of living in exchange for a depreciating dollar.

Because of the status of the dollar as the world's reserve currency, importing countries are willing to save in dollars and allow us to run trade deficits. And since these importing countries would prefer to save rather than purchase our goods and services, they are happy to lend these dollars back to us so we can buy more of their goods and services (which we can enjoy and use to further increase our standard of living).

Through this lens, the trade deficit seems not only innocuous, but beneficial. However, it is anything but benign. What we are really trading away is our income and our ability to save.

Our economy is measured as everything we produce. This is referred to as Gross Domestic Product (GDP). It can also be measured as everything we earn. This is referred to as Gross Domestic Income (GDI). GDP is always equal to GDI; whatever we produce is our income.

If we buy an imported product we have lowered our income by the amount of the import, and the exporting country's income has increased by the same amount. If we purchase more imports than we are exporting (a trade deficit), our income decreases and our economy will shrink (by the amount of the trade deficit).

The chart below shows our net trade as a percentage of GDP since 1948:

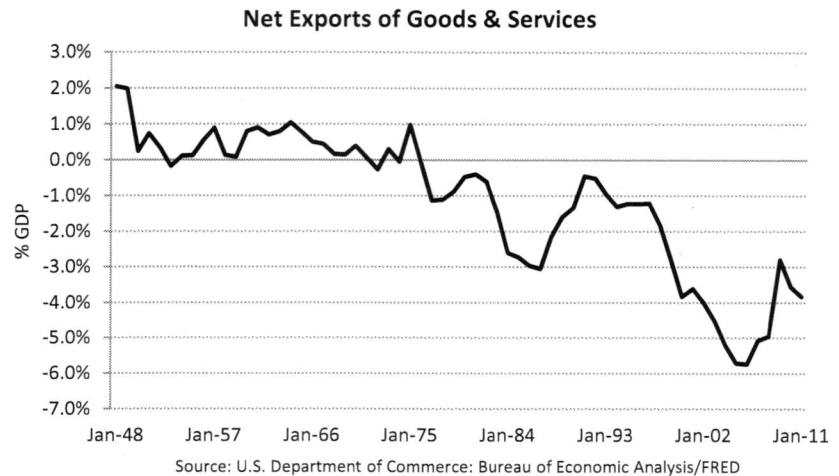

Until 1976, we generally ran a trade surplus. We were exporting more than we were importing and increasing our income and growing our economy through trade. In 1976, we started running a trade deficit, importing more than we were exporting, decreasing our income and shrinking our economy through trade.

In 1976, we basically had a zero net trade condition where imports equaled exports. If the balance of trade equals zero, and what you produce equals your income, then the only way to grow the economy is by deficit spending, which can be performed by the private or public (government) sectors.

The following accounting identity shows the effect of the sector actors on GDP:

Change in GDP = Government Deficit + Private Deficit + Trade Surplus

Without deficit spending (which includes spending prior years' savings), you can only have GDP growth through a trade surplus. If you are in a trade deficit, you must deficit spend in either the government or private sector to allow for GDP growth.

Below is a chart overlaying Net Trade and Net Government Spending as a percentage of GDP since 1948:

Net Trade, Net Government Spending

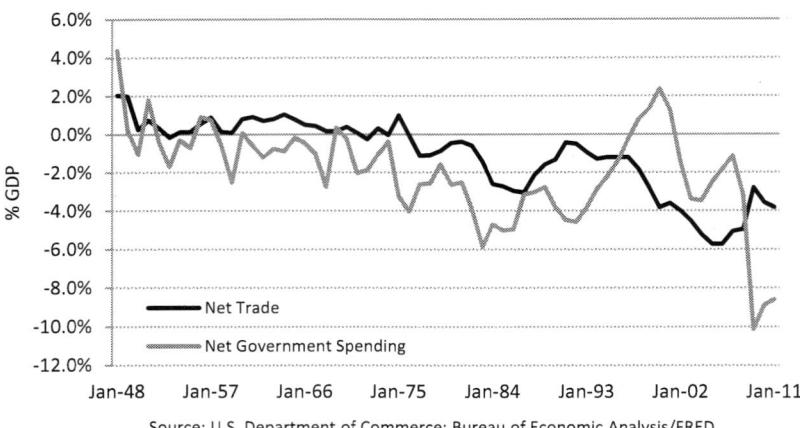

Source: U.S. Department of Commerce: Bureau of Economic Analysis/FRED

Up until 1996, the government deficit was always larger than the trade deficit (grey line below black line) unless we ran a trade surplus and government surplus at the same time (both grey and black lines are above 0%). So up until 1996, the government deficit spending made up for the loss of income to our economy from our trade deficits.

The chart below shows Net Trade minus Net Government Spending as a percentage of GDP since 1948:

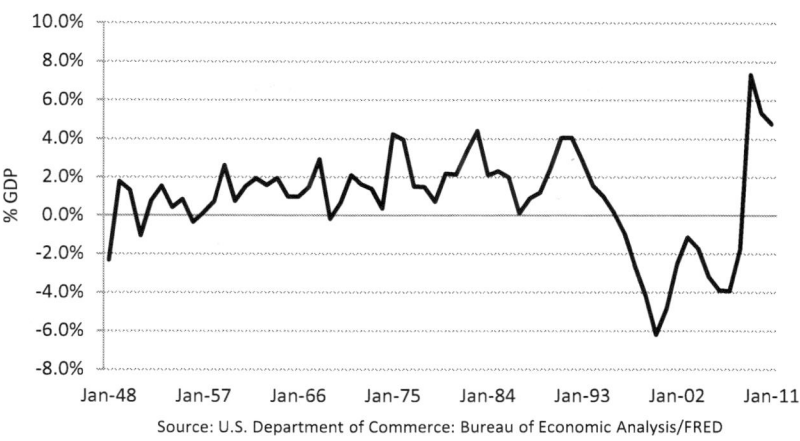

This chart shows the combined effect of net trade and net government spending on GDP. Up until 1996, this combination increased GDP (except in 1948, 1951, 1956 and 1969 when we were actually running a trade surplus, however, the government was running a larger surplus).

When the government runs a surplus (taxing more than it spends) it decreases GDP by an amount equal to the surplus (as this is lost income to the economy).

Most striking is what happens between 1996 and 2009 when the line on the graph rests significantly in negative territory. In these years government deficit spending was not making up for our trade deficit. The government ran a surplus between 1998 and 2002, which further reduced GDP and created the negative peak in 2000. The only avenue for GDP to grow between 1996 and 2009 was through private sector deficit spending.

The chart below overlays Net Trade minus Net Government Spending as a percentage of GDP against the percentage change in outstanding Consumer Debt per Laborer (inflation adjusted) since 1990:

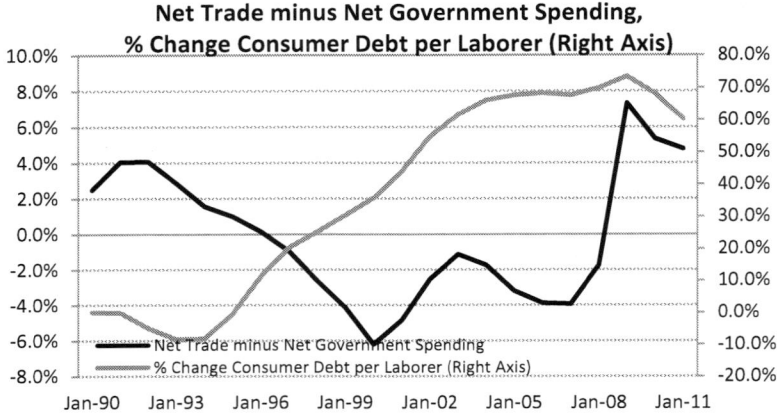

The private sector was required to significantly increase deficit spending as a result of the trade deficit. Between 1990 and 2006 the amount of inflation adjusted consumer debt owed per laborer increased by 68%. This debt was induced by the Federal Reserve lowering interest rates to pull in future purchases to increase aggregate demand and artificially keep the economy growing (as the non-wealthy private sector attempted to maintain their standard of living while real wages were decreasing).

By 2007, consumers were no longer able to take on additional debt to make up for the trade deficit and the economy entered a recession. In 2009, the government stepped in with massive government deficit spending (black line skyrockets from -2% to 7%) to not only make up for the trade deficit but to allow for consumers to start to save (grey line starts decline).

The chart below overlays Net Trade, Net Government Spending, and Net Private Spending as a percent of GDP since 1990:

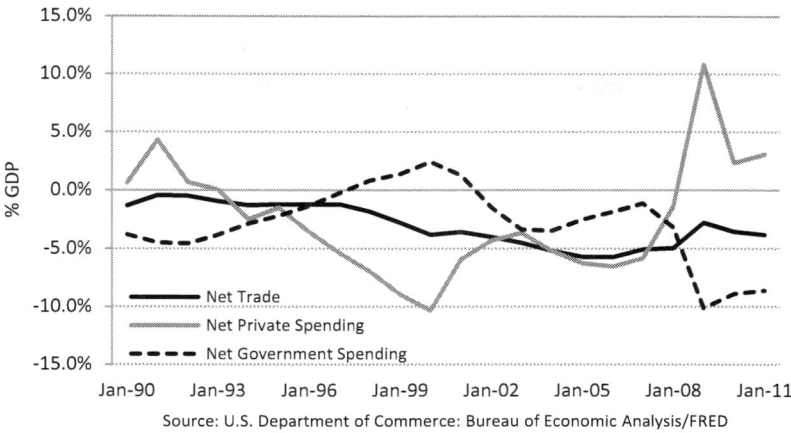

In 1996, when the government deficit was no longer making up for the trade deficit, the public sector had to start increasing their deficit spending. From 1998 to 2002 the private sector not only had to deficit spend to make up for the trade deficit, but also to make up for the government running a surplus (dotted-black line above zero).

From 2003 to 2007, the private sector deficit was almost exactly equal to the trade deficit (grey and solid-black lines overlap) and GDP growth was basically equal to government deficit spending.

In 2007, the public could no longer take on the additional debt needed to make up for the trade deficit (grey line broke above the solid-black line) and our economy entered a recession. In 2008, the public sector was only able to take on a small percentage of additional debt. As the public sector's deficit spending ability started to reduce the trade deficit also started to decrease (as we could no longer deficit spend to purchase imports).

By 2009, the private sector had reached its limit and was forced to be a net saver (grey line above zero) and start to pay down debt; this was enabled by massive government deficit spending (dotted-black line broke significantly below solid-black line), which ended the recession.

Since 2009, the private sector has continued to be in surplus (net savings) and the government sector has continued to massively deficit spend to allow the private sector to save, make up for the trade deficit, and provide modest GDP growth.

We can only run a trade deficit if our trading partners desire to save in U.S. dollars. When we run a trade deficit, it reduces our economy (GDP) and income by the exact amount of the deficit. To keep the economy from shrinking, we must then borrow back those dollars from our partner and use them to deficit spend (in the private and/or government sectors).

Though government deficit spending can make up for a trade deficit, government deficit spending is not good. A trade deficit is bad.

A surplus of government spending (taxing more than it spends) will reduce GDP by that amount. Therefore, paying down our national debt (through additional taxation) will reduce GDP. However, a trade surplus would allow an equal government surplus without reducing GDP.

The trade deficit is merely a symptom and a measure of the extent to which we are losing the global trade war. The root cause is a lack of global competitiveness, which is reducing our income and eroding our standard of living.

Chapter Two

Real Beasts of Debt Burden

Inflation, Distributions, Incentives, Distortions, Bigger Government

> *The drinks flow, people forget.*
> *That big wheel spins, the hair thins, people forget.*
> *Forget they're hiding.*
> *The news slows, people forget.*
> *That shares crash, hopes are dashed, people forget.*
> *Forget they're hiding.*
> *Behind an eminence front - an eminence front - it's a put-on.*
>
> "Eminence Front" – The Who

We cannot think of the national debt in the same way as we think of debt for an individual. The United States is a currency issuer whereas individuals (and States) are currency users. The United States can print the currency and individuals (and States) cannot.

When you are the currency issuer, technically, you can never default; you can just print more money to pay off your debts. Unlike an individual who has an end-of-life, the United States can rollover its debt indefinitely and never pay off the principle, which is what we do. Plus, we can create more debt to pay for the interest on the debt.

Today, we finance <u>some</u> of this debt through selling treasuries in the open market. The remaining debt is held in intergovernmental accounts or purchased by the Federal Reserve.

The chart below shows U.S. Treasury ownership by percentage between 2002 and 2010:

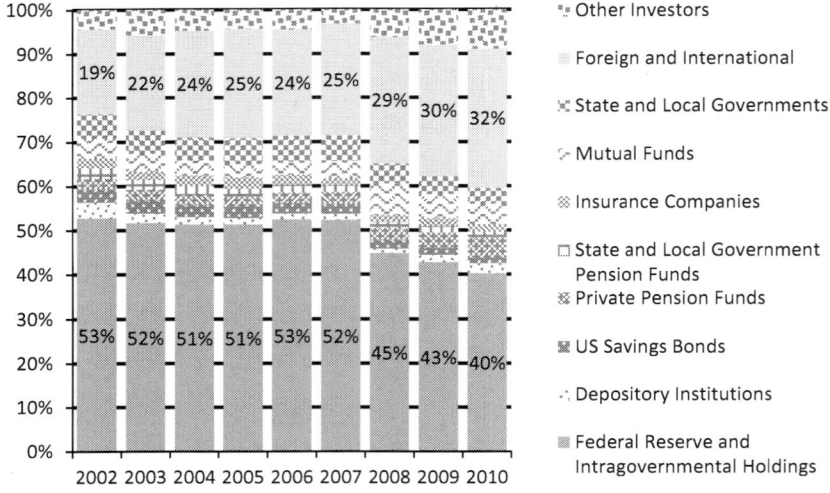

Currently we are only selling 60% of our debt into the open market (borrowing money). The Federal Reserve does not use borrowed money to purchase its portion, they merely press a button and deposit reserves (dollars) into the accounts of the Primary Dealers (the private banking institutions bestowed the privilege of selling treasuries for the U.S. Department of Treasury).

The quantitative easing programs are an example of the Federal Reserve purchasing treasuries by pressing a computer button and creating money out of thin air (modern day printing), which is deemed "monetizing" the debt. The U.S. Treasury pays interest on these treasuries to the Federal Reserve who then returns the interest to the U.S.

Treasury. It is purely printing money into existence for the U.S. government to deficit spend with no interest cost.

Though the share of the debt held by foreign investors is increasing, it accounts for only 32% of the total. Foreign holdings are broken down as follows:

United Kingdom	1%
Oil Exporters	2%
Japan	6%
China	9%
Other	<u>14%</u>
	32%

China holds 9% of our debt. The fear that China, who owns 9% of the debt, or any other foreign entity, will no longer purchase our debt and cause interest rates to skyrocket is unfounded given the monetization power of the Federal Reserve's printing press. The dollar will remain the world's reserve currency for the foreseeable future and there will continue to be significant demand from foreign countries to save in dollars.

U.S. treasuries are a carryover from when we were on the gold standard and the U.S. government actually had to borrow money to deficit spend. Through the qualitative easing programs, Federal Reserve Chairman Ben Bernanke has thoroughly debunked the myth that we must borrow to deficit spend.

We still sell <u>some</u> treasuries on the open market, but we will never have a failed treasury auction (debt sale). The Primary Dealers, are never at risk of not being able to sell the treasuries because the Federal Reserve will ensure that the sale is successful by buying any treasuries they need to (monetizing the debt), or, by incentivizing the banks to hold the debt at a profit.

The Primary Dealers can never lose and there will never be a failed auction. Let's not forget, the Primary Dealers (Goldman Sachs, Merrill Lynch, JP Morgan, Citigroup, etc.) are member-owners of the Federal Reserve.

The primary mechanism used by the Federal Reserve to control interest rates is the purchasing (monetizing) of U.S. treasuries. The Federal Reserve typically only seeks to control short-term rates through the purchase of short-term treasuries. By setting the rate for "risk-free" short-term treasuries, the Federal Reserve can influence all competing rates. By targeting lower interest rates the Federal Reserve can increase the demand for money and stoke the economy. By targeting higher interest rates (which is accomplished by the Federal Reserve selling some of its Treasury holdings) the Federal Reserve can reduce the demand for money and cool the economy.

In normal times, the longer-term interest rates are determined primarily by the market and are largely influenced by inflation expectations. However, now that we are in a "liquidity trap" (where the Federal Reserve targeted rate is 0% and can no longer be lowered to increase the demand for money), the Federal Reserve has been targeting lower longer-term interest rates as well by purchasing longer-term treasuries through Operation Twist (increasing the average maturity of the treasuries they hold and reducing the average maturity of treasuries in the open market).

The following chart shows the maturity distribution of the debt held by private investors (2011 data, Office of Debt Management, Office of the Under Secretary for Domestic Finance):

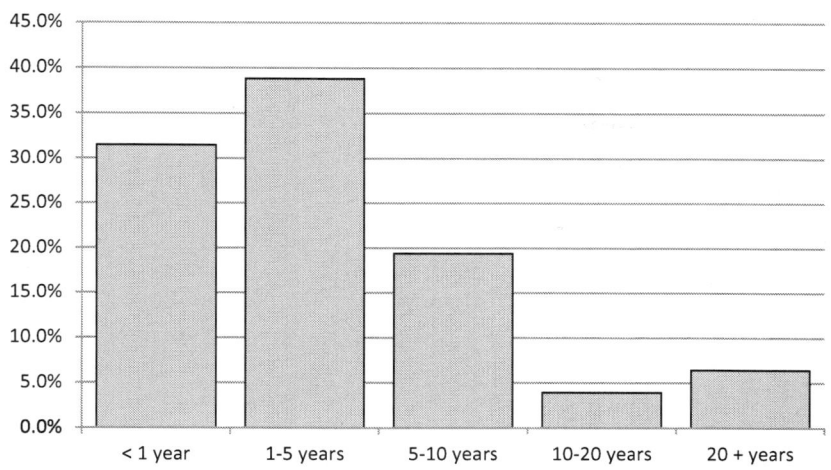

The average length of debt outstanding is 60 months.

Though the Federal Reserve uses treasuries to control interest rates, they have other tools that they could use instead such as paying interest on excess reserves. The Federal Reserve monetizes the interest payments on excess reserves by pressing a button just as it does to purchase treasuries. And though we could eliminate treasuries, the resulting interest payments for any method would be similar (as this is really the underlying force employed).

However, monetization is not a free lunch; as running the printing press to create dollars ultimately leads to inflation which subjects financial repression upon those who must work (and are losing their purchasing power) to the benefit of those who are wealthy and own the assets.

Government deficit spending results in higher taxes to service the interest payments. 53% of the interest payments for our debt is going to foreigners and 47% is going to Americans. More specifically, it is the wealthy who own the majority of the assets, including treasuries, so 53% of our interest payments are going to wealthy foreigners and 47% of our interest payments are going to wealthy Americans. This interest is primarily paid by those in the U.S. who have to work (and pay income taxes).

When working people are taxed to pay the interest on the debt they are transferring their ability to purchase resources to those who are wealthy and own the debt. Deficit spending today will cause our children who will have to work in the future to transfer their ability to purchase resources to those who are wealthy. This tax on labor will create a disincentive on performing productivity activity.

Deficit spending (along with its partner in financial repression - inflation) has been a principle cause of the destruction of the middle class and for widening of the wealth gap by allowing the federal government to increase in size.

Government spending (and deficit spending) disproportionately benefits the elite class who are able to influence the governors to the detriment of those who must work. The bigger the government, the greater the distortions and the greater the inequity between those who can afford to influence the governors and those who are subject to working. This feedback loop then allows the lobbyist's benefactors to donate to the political campaigns of the governors whom they influence.

The distortions provide advantages to the elite through subsidies, regulations, earmarks and government programs; and creates incentives to invest in non-productive capital to game the system while limiting competition and discouraging those not in the privileged position to be benefactors.

Once additional government is created, it is in the interest of those who are hired into the public positions to protect their existence versus creating efficiencies; there is no free market competition within the government. These distortions make the economy less efficient and less productive, lowering our standard of living. Government itself is not competing within a system of capitalism; it is distorting the private markets into crony capitalism.

Unfortunately the federal government, by its very nature, distorts the marketplace in favor of the wealthy. The best we can do is minimize the role of the federal government and try to move the powers as close as possible to people (local and state governments). Our forefathers absolutely intended a limited role of the federal government as they clearly understood our corruptible nature as well as the inevitability of even well-intentioned people to create unintended consequences.

The national debt matters, but not for the reasons that most people think. The debt itself creates issues of inflation, distributions, incentives, and distortions. However, the most egregious effect of the debt is that it enables a bigger federal government, which creates additional distortions that benefit the elite and lowers our standard of living by reducing our productivity.

As the currency issuer, the U.S. can never technically default on the debt as we have the power to print money to make debt payments. We never need to pay back the debt principal and can issue more debt to make the interest payments. We do not even need to issue debt to deficit spend as the Federal Reserve can and does print money to purchase treasuries.

Government deficit spending increases inflation, which subjects financial repression upon those who must work (and are losing their purchasing power) to the benefit of those who are wealthy and own the assets.

The interest payments on the debt transfers the ability to purchase goods and services from those Americans who must work to the wealthy foreigners and wealthy Americans who are the debt holders.

Debt causes the marginal tax rate to increase on working people and acts as a disincentive to productive activity, which causes GDP to decrease; which causes an even higher increase in marginal tax rates on the working people and a vicious circle of ever-decreasing productivity.

The most detrimental effect of deficit spending is that it enables the size of the federal government to increase.

The government creates distortions in the market to the benefit of the special interest groups who are lobbying them; creating the financial feedback loop which funds donations to the politician's campaigns.

The bigger the federal government, the greater the distortion to the markets, the lower our productivity, and the lower our standard of living.

Chapter Three

The Duke of Moral Hazard

> *We're off to see the Wizard,*
> *The Wonderful Wizard of Oz,*
> *We hear he is a whiz of a Wiz,*
> *If ever, oh ever a Wiz there was.*
> *The Wizard of Oz is one because,*
> *Because, because, because, because, because,*
> *Because of the wonderful things he does.*
> *We're off to see the Wizard,*
> *The Wonderful Wizard of Oz.*
>
> *"We're Off to See the Wizard"* – Harold Arlen

Inflation is the result of the money supply growing faster than the economy and is purposely engineered by the Federal Reserve. The money supply can only be increased in one of two ways.

One way money can be created is for the Federal Reserve to monetize the debt (treasuries) or purchase other assets.

> Note: when the Federal Reserve purchases an asset that is not backed by the full faith and credit of the U.S. government it is engaging in fiscal policy, a power only to be possessed by Congress, as there can be a loss on the asset, which is transferred to the U.S. taxpayer. Since the financial crisis, the Federal Reserve has purchased a significant amount of assets (many of which would be deemed "toxic") to bail out the banking system. Congress should be outraged by the Federal Reserve engaging in fiscal policy (as the Federal Reserve is only authorized to engage in monetary policy).

If the Federal Reserve were to buy an asset, but at the same time sell an asset of equal value that it had already purchased, this would not increase the money supply and this process is called "sterilization." So any unsterilized purchase by the Federal Reserve increases the money supply as they simple press a button to print money into existence to purchase the asset.

The second way money can be created is by banks who have the privilege of operating a fractional reserve system. The rules of the system mathematically limit the banks' ability to create money, however, the reality is that the banks are never reserve restrained and can create an unlimited amount of money only subject to capital requirements. This is because they can borrow excess reserves from other banks and if there are no excess reserves to be borrowed they can get temporary loans from the Federal Reserve. And once the banks create a new loan, excess reserves are created in the system, which they can then borrow. Like the Federal Reserve, our banks also have the power of the printing press (this is free money that they create for which they pay no interest). And let's not forget, it is our banks who own the Federal Reserve.

To keep prices stable, the money supply does have to grow with the population and economic activity. However, within the control of the quantity of money, inflation must be minimized as it causes financial repression.

Wikipedia defines "financial repression" as follows:

> "Newly printed money can be used to purchase goods and services, and to discharge debts, at no cost to the printer. This acts as a mechanism to transfer the wealth of society to those that can print money, from everyone else. Financial repression is most successful in

liquidating debts when accompanied by a steady dose of inflation, and it can be considered a form of taxation."

John Maynard Keynes, warning about the menaces of inflation, stated:

"By a continuous process of inflation, governments can confiscate, secretly and unobserved, an important part of the wealth of their citizens. By this method, they not only confiscate, but they confiscate arbitrarily; and while the process impoverishes many, it actually enriches some."

Unfortunately, the Federal Reserve now believes more inflation is better as it will reduce the burden of our debt and depreciate the dollar, which will make our goods more globally competitive and increase exports. By depreciating the dollar, the Federal Reserve is, in stealth, reducing our wages, which results in less purchasing power for American workers and an increase in profitability for corporations.

Inflation does allow the Federal Reserve more flexibility in using interest rates to influence the demand for money. For as their targeted rate reaches zero (like it is today), the Federal Reserve can no longer further lower interest rates to increase the demand for money; this is deemed a "liquidity trap." The Federal Reserve uses inflation as a vehicle to allow interest rates to remain in a positive territory so they have room to decrease rates and increase the demand for money without reaching the lower bound of zero and entering a liquidity trap. However, it was complete mismanagement by the Federal Reserve that put us in this current untenable liquidity trap situation.

The Federal Reserve produces the targeted inflation level by controlling the supply of money through manipulating interest rates via the purchase of treasuries to meet its dual mandate of price stability and full employment. Their methods achieve price stability based on a targeted inflation level. To the Federal Reserve, price stability paradoxically requires inflation.

We are in a liquidity trap because even at the lowest rate possible (zero), the Federal Reserve cannot induce people to spend or take on new debt because their discretionary spending has reached its limit. This was caused by Alan Greenspan's actions as Federal Reserve Chairman engineering what was deemed the "Great Moderation" (which claimed the success of eliminating volatility in the business cycle and tempering recessions).

During the Great Moderation, each time the economy started to slow, the Federal Reserve models indicated that inflation was relatively low (as there was low demand from the slowing economy) so the Federal Reserve lowered interest rates to increase demand for money, which created aggregate demand for goods and services and spurred the economy. These actions worked by pulling forward demand (buying capacity) from the future and allowed the Federal Reserve to claim perceived success for a continually growing economy.

However, the Federal Reserve's models did not account for the increase in private sector debt that was accumulating and how much its servicing requirements would affect future demand. Today we are in the future and we are paying for the debt issued in the past, which was pulled forward by the actions of the Federal Reserve.

Each Federal Reserve intervention created additional unintended consequences. Besides the unforeseen draining of future demand, loose money fueled uncontrollable asset bubbles. These asset bubbles absorbed the new money being created and were a covert form of inflation. In addition, the asset bubbles made people feel wealthy and capable of taking on more debt, which further spurred malinvestment; we continue to service these debts, which is why we remain in a liquidity trap.

Hubris played a significant role in the Federal Reserve believing that "this time is different" and that they had mastered the economy and the ability to create Goldilocks outcomes. The reality is that we relied on debt to beget debt with no consideration to the fact that this could not go on ad infinitum.

During the Great Moderation, savings was disincentivized through low rates and the belief that savings were no longer necessary as we could rely on consistent growth and perpetual prosperity. No consideration was given to the effect on future outcomes as we knew that the great wizard at the Federal Reserve could always engineer the desired result.

Greenspan's encouragement of investors to take risk at the bequest of the Federal Reserve institutionalized moral hazard as standard dogma and was coined the "Greenspan Put;" investors could not lose with the Federal Reserve at the wheel. This further spurred bubbles and malinvestment.

The Federal Reserve created significant distortions in the market with unpredictable and unintended consequences. Their actions created self-reinforcing bubbles that when popped caused the Federal Reserve to become even more accommodative and create even bigger unintended bubbles. The Federal Reserve's belief that they could eliminate volatility in the business cycle created significantly greater volatility to the extent to where they can no longer lower rates to try to engineer their next soft landing and are forced to use increasingly blunt instruments to implement monetary policy that will undoubtedly create even more disastrous unintended consequences.

In 1966, psychologist Abraham Maslow stated, "I suppose it is tempting, if the only tool you have is a hammer, to treat everything as if it were a nail." I supposed it is very tempting when all you have is the unauditable monopoly power of money creation, to treat every economic problem as if it can be solved with a printing press.

Inflation causes "financial repression" as it disproportionately penalizes those who must work by reducing the purchasing power of their wages to the benefit of the wealthy who own the assets.

Paradoxically, the Federal Reserve targets inflation to create "price stability" as it cannot lower interest rates below the zero bound. Therefore, we do not have price stability, but, have a stable rate of the reduction in the value of the purchasing power of money.

When demand slows in the economy, the standard inflation measures are naturally low. The Federal Reserve took this as a green light that it was safe to keep rates low to increase aggregate demand. These actions pulled forward demand and growth from the future through the accumulation of unsustainable debt.

The Federal Reserve did not understand the modern avenues of inflation and their loose money policies created asset bubbles, which spurred speculation and malinvestment in non-productive capital.

The popping of these asset bubbles solicited greater monetary easing responses from the Federal Reserve, which created even bigger asset bubbles and greater responses to where we have entered a liquidity trap; such that even with interest rates at zero, their lower bound, we can no longer induce

people to increase spending or take on new debts as they have reached their limit servicing past advances.

Through encouraging the accumulation of debt and facilitating speculation in malinvestments the Federal Reserve mortgaged our future growth and continues to pursue policies that increasingly distort markets and will likely result in unpredictable and extremely negative outcomes.

Chapter Four

Private Sectored

You may find yourself living in a shotgun shack,
And you may find yourself in another part of the world,
And you may find yourself behind the wheel of a large automobile,
And you may find yourself in a beautiful house, with a beautiful wife,
And you may ask yourself, well, how did I get here?
Letting the days go by let the water hold me down,
Letting the days go by water flowing underground,
Into the blue again after the money's gone,
Once in a lifetime water flowing underground.
And you may ask yourself, how do I work this?
And you may ask yourself, where is that large automobile?
And you may tell yourself, this is not my beautiful house!
And you may tell yourself, this is not my beautiful wife!

"Once in a Lifetime" – Talking Heads

Gross Domestic Product (GDP) and Gross Domestic Income (GDI) are equal and encompass basic accounting identities that state whatever we produce becomes our income. As long as the demand for saving and borrowing is equal, the economy will stay at the same level. If spending is greater than income through either spending prior years' savings or borrowing to spend, the economy will grow. If there is more demand to save than to borrow (and spend) the economy will shrink. The Federal Reserve and banks can print money into existence to accommodate deficit spending. For our economy to grow, we must deficit spend more than we save. Note: we will ignore the effects of trade (imports/exports) for this discussion.

This is the point in the logic chain where everyone starts going off the tracks. The next jump they make is that for us to have net private sector savings without shrinking the economy, the government must deficit spend. This is true, but leads to the completely false conclusion that the private sector cannot save without the government deficit spending. Furthermore, it leads to the incorrect interpretation that government deficit spending is necessary and the more the government deficit spends the better, as it will increase the private sector's net savings. This is absolutely wrong and an extremely dangerous misinterpretation!

People instinctively know that private sector saving is good, however, they improperly expand this belief to assume that net private sector saving is good. They get confounded between their instincts being correct that it is good to save and incorrectly believe that we need net private sector savings to allow people to save (which is why government deficit spending is incorrectly believed to be good).

GDP and GDI create account balance identities that are merely a single snapshot in time of the aggregate and this concept is vastly misunderstood.

Let's think about a world where the population and demographics are constant, there is no inflation, we have full employment and everyone is getting the goods and services that they desire. It would be just fine for the economy to stay at the same level. It would be nice if more goods and services (or leisure time) could be provided that people could enjoy and that would be accomplished through productivity improvements not an increased measure of GDP/GDI.

People in this world would still think saving is good. And we are usually always saving in some form (401ks, pension plans, investments, building home equity, life insurance, etc.). However, though we may be saving, the reality is that we usually start our working lives with a negative balance sheet. We take out loans for our education, homes and vehicles, and then as our salaries increase and we have more buying power we may upgrade homes or perhaps be lucky enough to pay for our children's education.

As we generally begin our working lives not owning anything, we leverage our future earning potential by taking on debt to buy what we need and make investments (though we are usually saving in several forms at the same time). Over time, we pay down our debt and at some point have a positive balance sheet. We then continue to build our savings until we retire at which time we become pure spenders.

In this balanced world, when we want to appropriately save there is someone else who is at the point of their life where it is appropriate to borrow our savings to spend. In addition, there are willing workers to create the goods and services that are desired by everyone including those who are retired.

If the population were growing, we would be adding more young people who start off as debtors and the economy (GDP/GDI) would grow through their additional deficit spending (without the need for the government to deficit spend). It would be perfectly healthy to have a net private sector deficit as the economy grew to absorb the productivity of these new workers.

Let's now take our example economy and evaluate what is happening today from the effects of deficit spending. For simplicity, we'll use an example of someone who, in our closed system, wants to deficit spend more than the savings that are available.

Let's suppose someone wants to buy a piece of land and the owner agrees to sell it to him for $10,000. The buyer then goes to the bank to secure a $10,000 loan and the bank prints the money into existence and deposits it into the land seller's bank account. The terms of the loan are that the buyer will pay $1,000 in principal each year for 10 years with 10% interest.

The chart below shows what happens during the life of the loan.

	Money Creation	Principal Payment	Interest Payment	Buyer's Balance Sheet	Buyer's Savings	Seller's Savings	Bank's Savings	Net Private Sector Savings	Change GDP/GDI
Year 0	$10,000			-$10,000	-$10,000			-$10,000	$10,000
Year 1	-$1,000	$1,000	$1,000	-$9,000	$1,000	$10,000		$11,000	-$11,000
Year 2	-$1,000	$1,000	$900	-$8,000	$1,000		$1,000	$2,000	-$2,000
Year 3	-$1,000	$1,000	$800	-$7,000	$1,000		$900	$1,900	-$1,900
Year 4	-$1,000	$1,000	$700	-$6,000	$1,000		$800	$1,800	-$1,800
Year 5	-$1,000	$1,000	$600	-$5,000	$1,000		$700	$1,700	-$1,700
Year 6	-$1,000	$1,000	$500	-$4,000	$1,000		$600	$1,600	-$1,600
Year 7	-$1,000	$1,000	$400	-$3,000	$1,000		$500	$1,500	-$1,500
Year 8	-$1,000	$1,000	$300	-$2,000	$1,000		$400	$1,400	-$1,400
Year 9	-$1,000	$1,000	$200	-$1,000	$1,000		$300	$1,300	-$1,300
Year 10	-$1,000	$1,000	$100	$0	$1,000		$200	$1,200	-$1,200
Year 11							$100	$100	-$100
	$0	$10,000	$5,500		$0	$10,000	$5,500	$15,500	-$15,500

At Year 0, the point of the sale, the land buyer deficit spends $10,000 and the land seller has an additional $10,000 of income. During this year, the economy has grown by $10,000 and there is a net private sector deficit of $10,000 (the equivalent of the increase of the economy).

In Year 1, the purchaser pays the bank $1,000 in principal and $1,000 in interest for the loan. Just as the bank printed $10,000 into existence the prior year when they created the loan, they now destroy the $1,000 principal payment from existence. The $1,000 interest payment is income to the bank (which substituted for a different purchase the land buyer could have made with the money). The land seller was already receiving all of the goods and services that he had desired (not changing from before the land sale) and does not spend his $10,000. So in Year 1, the economy is reduced by $11,000, $10,000 that the land seller did not spend and $1,000 from the destruction of the principal payment (which the land buyer could not spend).

In Year 2, the purchaser again makes the $1,000 principal payment, which is destroyed by the bank and pays $900 in interest to the bank. The bank distributed their prior years' income of $1,000 to their stock holders who already had enough income from before this loan, so this became additional savings for them. Therefore, the economy is reduced by $2000; $1,000 for the principal that is destroyed and $1,000 from the bank owner's saving their additional income.

In year 0, the economy grew by the amount of the private sector deficit spending (the loan). Every year that the debt of the loan was being serviced, the economy decreased by the amount of the net private sector savings. After the loan was completely serviced, the economy (GDP/GDI) had been reduced by $15,500.

The net effect of the loan being taken out is that the total economic activity decreased by $15,500 and the net private sector savings increased by $15,500. The year the loan was initiated there was growth in the economy and for the next ten years the economy was in recession!

The purchase of this land created net private sector savings, which reduced the economy by the same amount. Should we then conclude that we need government deficit spending to allow for net private sector savings? No, the real question we must ask is; why is there net private sector savings? The economy was doing just fine when we had zero net private sector savings.

In this example, the years that the loan was outstanding the economy was no longer healthy and balanced, it was in a Balance Sheet Recession. The person who took out the loan had less purchasing power while they were paying off their loan and their impaired balance sheet reduced the economy by the exact amount of their total loss of purchasing power. The purchasing power of the land buyer was completely transferred to the land owner and the bank owners. And the savings of the land seller and the bank owners were equal to the reduction in the economy.

However, we are incorrectly stating that it is a Balance Sheet Recession. From acquiring the loan, the land buyer's balance sheet was impaired by $10,000. But, the land seller's balance sheet grew by $10,000! After the loan was fully paid off, the land buyer had a zero balance sheet, the land seller had $10,000 and the bank owners had $5,500. The combination of which, $15,500, is the total reduction of the economy.

This scenario created a Balance Sheet Recession because the land owner and the bank owners did not spend their savings. So, the person who had no more discretionary buying power (the land buyer) was balance sheet impaired and the economy went into recession. It was not a net private sector balance sheet issue.

This scenario represents exactly what we are experiencing today. The real problem is that the income is being disproportionately distributed to the wealthy (illustrated by the land owner and bank owners in this example) who do not desire to spend their income. The wealthy do not think of savings as savings per se; they use their savings to generate their income (versus having to work).

The table below shows the percent of income earned by the Top 10% of Earners since 1970 (Piketty-Saez):

Percentage of Income Earned by Top 10% from 1970 – 2010

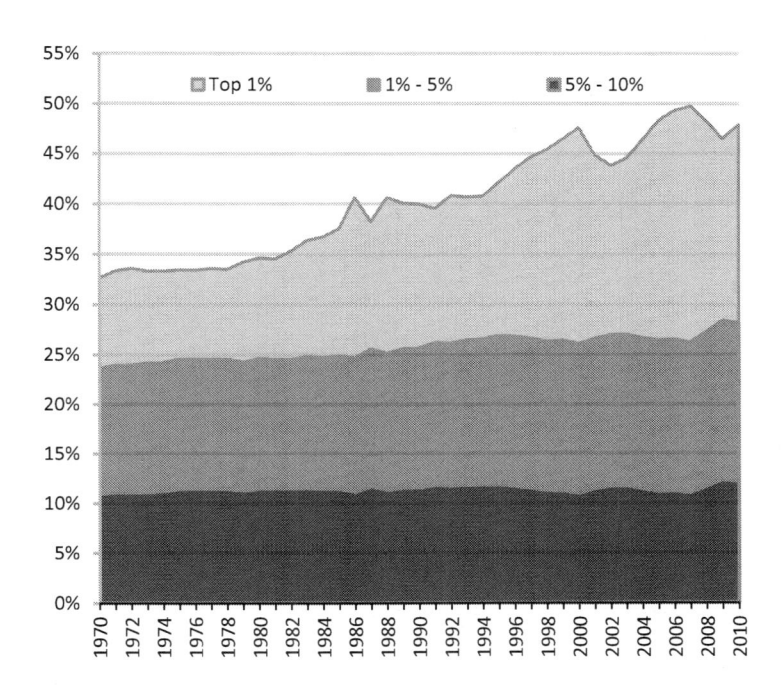

As more of the income is being distributed to the wealthy the economy is reduced by the amount of their savings. It is a misnomer to say that we are in a private sector balance sheet recession. The reality is that the desire of the wealthy to save can no longer be absorbed as deficit spending by those who must work and have reached their debt limit (as they have borrowed to try to maintain their standard of living as their real wages have not kept up with inflation). The net private sector balance sheet is in the green (positive).

We have an unbalanced system where the wealthy people are generating more savings than the workers can take on in new debt.

Let's now take a look at what would have happened if the $10,000 loan (deficit spending) had been used to purchase an import rather than spend domestically, as shown in the chart below:

	Money Creation	Principal Payment	Interest Payment	Buyer's Balance Sheet	Buyer's Savings	Foreign Savings	Foreign Bank's Savings	Net Private Sector Savings	Change GDP/GDI
Year 0	10,000			-10,000	-10,000				
Year 1	-1,000	1,000	1,000	-9,000	1,000	10,000			-2,000
Year 2	-1,000	1,000	900	-8,000	1,000		1,000		-1,900
Year 3	-1,000	1,000	800	-7,000	1,000		900		-1,800
Year 4	-1,000	1,000	700	-6,000	1,000		800		-1,700
Year 5	-1,000	1,000	600	-5,000	1,000		700		-1,600
Year 6	-1,000	1,000	500	-4,000	1,000		600		-1,500
Year 7	-1,000	1,000	400	-3,000	1,000		500		-1,400
Year 8	-1,000	1,000	300	-2,000	1,000		400		-1,300
Year 9	-1,000	1,000	200	-1,000	1,000		300		-1,200
Year 10	-1,000	1,000	100	0	1,000		200		-1,100
Year 11							100		
	0	10,000	5,500	0	10,000	5,500			-15,500

The net effect of reducing the economy by $15,500 is exactly the same! However, in this case wealthy foreigners are able to save the same $15,500 versus wealthy Americans. There is no difference in the effect of wealthy foreigners and wealthy Americans wanting to save in dollars.

When the population is increasing, it is normal and healthy to be running small private sector deficits that increase the economy. However, there has been a dearth of the middle class and a widening of income inequality in the U.S. to such an extent that we should now think of there being two distinct private sectors; the non-wealthy majority and the wealthy minority.

In 1996 the non-wealthy private sector started to take on debt at unsustainable levels which began to increasingly impair their balance sheets. In 2007, the non-wealthy private sector had surpassed its limit to take on more debt and we entered into what was coined a Balance Sheet Recession. And though today the economy is growing modestly through massive government deficit spending, the non-wealthy private sector still has an impaired balance sheet and is working to pay down debt (deleverage).

Let's look at what would have happened if the land seller and bank owners' had spent their income and kept the money in the economy, as shown in the chart below.

	Money Creation	Principal Payment	Interest Payment	Buyer's Balance Sheet	Buyer's Savings	Seller's Savings	Bank's Savings	Net Private Sector Savings	Change GDP/GDI
Year 0	10,000			-10,000	-10,000			-10,000	10,000
Year 1	-1,000	1,000	1,000	-9,000	1,000			1,000	-1,000
Year 2	-1,000	1,000	900	-8,000	1,000			1,000	-1,000
Year 3	-1,000	1,000	800	-7,000	1,000			1,000	-1,000
Year 4	-1,000	1,000	700	-6,000	1,000			1,000	-1,000
Year 5	-1,000	1,000	600	-5,000	1,000			1,000	-1,000
Year 6	-1,000	1,000	500	-4,000	1,000			1,000	-1,000
Year 7	-1,000	1,000	400	-3,000	1,000			1,000	-1,000
Year 8	-1,000	1,000	300	-2,000	1,000			1,000	-1,000
Year 9	-1,000	1,000	200	-1,000	1,000			1,000	-1,000
Year 10	-1,000	1,000	100	0	1,000			1,000	-1,000
Year 11									
	0	10,000	5,500		0			0	0

In this case the economy was increased at the time of the purchase by the amount of the deficit spending. Then in the following 10 years, while the loan was being serviced, the economy was in recession as it was being reduced by amount of the loan principal payment. After the loan was completely serviced there was no net change to the level of the economy or to net private sector savings. In this scenario, the only effect of the purchase was to pull forward demand (as was encouraged by the wizards of the Federal Reserve), which increased the economy in the year of the purchase and then led to a ten year economic recession.

The private sector income is disproportionally distributed to the wealthy as there has been a dilution of the middle class. And we can now think of America as having two private

sectors; the non-wealthy majority, who through government distortions and inflation, have lost the purchasing power of their wages and have impaired balance sheets, and the wealthy minority who have the majority of the income, significantly positive balance sheets (wealth) and are not spending their savings, which is causing the economy to contract.

The government is now massively deficit spending to allow the wealthy to maintain their rate of savings (as the non-wealthy private sector can no longer take on the debt to absorb it) while providing for modest economic growth.

Our Trade Deficit problem can be thought of as a productivity issue with the beneficiary being wealthy foreigners who desire to save in dollars. And our Private Sector Balance Sheet Recession problem can be thought of as an income distribution distortion issue with the beneficiary being wealthy Americans who also desire to save in dollars.

Chapter Five

Trade Enemy Within

I watched with glee while your kings and queens,
Fought for ten decades for the gods they made.
I shouted out - who killed the Kennedys?
When after all it was you and me.
Let me please introduce myself, I'm a man of wealth and taste.
And I laid traps for troubadours who get killed before they reached Bombay.
Pleased to meet you - hope you guessed my name,
But what's puzzling you is the nature of my game.

"Sympathy for the Devil" - The Rolling Stones

Every country cannot be a net exporter and enjoy its benefits of additional income, growth, and the ability to save. Global trade must balance to net zero across all nations.

In 2011, the United States had a trade deficit with 101 countries and a trade surplus with 136 countries. However, our net trade was a $579 billion deficit, which reduced our economy and income by 3.8% of GDP (though a massive government spending deficit of 8.6% of GDP allowed for modest growth of 1.7%).

In 2011, our top 10 deficit trading partners accounted for 85% of the trade deficit:

	Country	% of Trade Deficit
1.	China	34%
2.	Mexico	12%
3.	Canada	9%
4.	Japan	7%
5.	Germany	6%
6.	Ireland	4%
7.	Saudi Arabia	4%
8.	Nigeria	3%
9.	Venezuela	3%
10.	Russia	3%
		85%

We import 49% of our oil demand. In 2011, we imported $392 billion of oil, which was 15% of our total imports and would represent 68% of the trade deficit. The top 11 oil importers accounted for 82% of all oil imports.

	Country	% of Oil Imports
1.	Canada	24%
2.	Mexico	11%
3.	Saudi Arabia	11%
4.	Venezuela	8%
5.	Nigeria	7%
6.	Russia	5%
7.	Iraq	4%
8.	Colombia	4%
9.	Algeria	3%
10.	Angola	3%
11.	Brazil	2%
		82%

If we could resolve our energy needs so that we did not need to import oil, we could reduce our trade deficit by 68%. And though the numbers point us in that direction, it is a very dangerous conclusion that we should attack the trade deficit through oil independence.

When we entrusted the government to provide such a solution, they made this same jeopardous conclusion and implemented ethanol subsidies through the Volumetric Ethanol Excise Tax Credit (VEETC), which was part of the American Jobs Creation Act of 2004. The VEETC existed until the end of 2011 and provided $54 billion in ethanol subsidies.

In addition, the Energy Policy Act of 2005 required a Renewable Fuel Standard of 4 billion gallons by 2006, 6.1 billion gallons by 2007 and 7.5 billion by 2012. Two years later the Energy Independence and Security Act of 2007 extended the target to 9 billion gallons by 2008 and 36 billion gallons by 2022.

Though the VEETC expired at the end of 2011 and we are no longer paying a direct subsidy for ethanol, the special interest groups had already been guaranteed indirect subsidies through the Renewable Fuel Standard mandates and the market distortions continue at an even greater rate.

In 2012, it is expected that 38% of the corn grown in the U.S. will be used in biofuel production, which will consume 33 million acres of farmland. Since 2005, when the ethanol subsidies began, corn prices have tripled and all food costs have increased through the distortions of the markets. We have provided billions in grants and loan guarantees to biofuel producers who have predominantly ended up in bankruptcy.

When originally proposed, ethanol was promised to enhance our national security by reducing our dependence on volatile oil producing nations and was touted as an economically friendly oil alternative that would reduce green house gas emissions; neither turned out to be true.

Ethanol subsidies have created significant unintended distortions, which have increased the price of food and other commodities.

There are many countries in the world that can produce energy (oil) and ship it to us at a lower cost than we can make it ourselves. They have a competitive advantage in the energy market and we should take advantage of their lower energy prices by purchasing their products.

We should not try to counteract the oil imports by distorting the energy markets through government subsidies or regulations. These market distortions only benefit the special interest groups who profit directly from them and hurt America as a whole.

As world demand for oil increases and as lower cost sources are depleted, oil prices will increase and free and undistorted markets will adjust most efficiently to the changing energy prices. People will change their behaviors and oil substitutes will be created to provide for people's energy needs. We cannot predict the best potential solution (as there will be new technologies available for which we still have no visibility), nor should we mandate one, as we will only be wasting resources through malinvestment.

To counteract the energy trade imbalance (or any trade imbalance), we must increase our productivity and create competitive advantages so that other countries will purchase our goods because we can produce them more economically. These must be higher value-add goods that require advanced technologies and skills, and will justify greater wage compensation and provide Americans an improved standard of living. We should not try to distort markets (with subsidies and regulations) to compete with other countries who have

natural competitive advantages; this will only reduce our productivity through malinvestment.

Though OPEC influences the price of oil through regulating supply by member producers, we are freely competing with other countries for this source of energy and the price of oil is determined based on its aggregate supply and demand. On the other hand, we are not freely competing with China who has been significantly manipulating our trade dynamics to where they are importing 4.1 times the amount we are exporting to them and our trade deficit with China represents 34% of our total trade deficit.

<u>China's Trade Distortion Mechanisms</u>
- Currency Manipulation
- Tariffs
- Forced Partnerships
- Forced Technology Transfers
- Domestic Content Requirements
- Predatory Pricing (Dumping)
- Non-Enforcement of Intellectual Property Laws
- Labor Force Exploitation
- Environmental Exploitation
- Government Subsidies

China manipulates their currency by pegging the renminbi to the dollar (its value is not determined by the free market) as they have been waging economic war on the United States for over 20 years.

The following chart shows the effect of the trade deficit with China on GDP since 1985 (grey shaded sections highlight U.S. recessions):

China Trade Deficit as % of US GDP

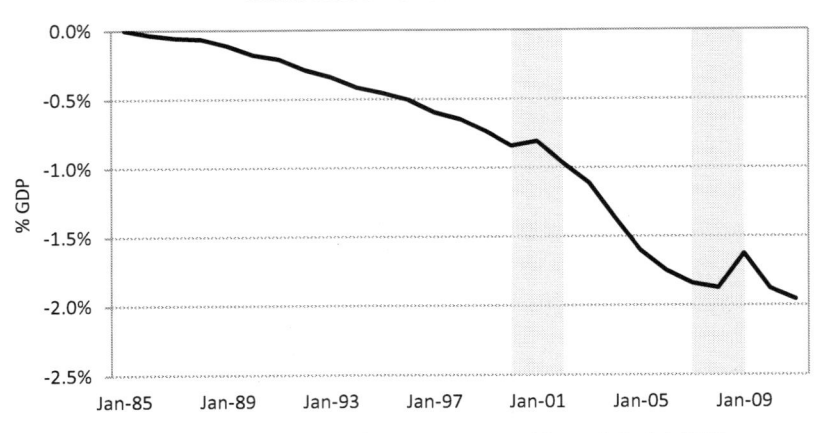

Source: U.S. Department of Commerce: Bureau of Economic Analysis/FRED

The trade deficit with China is currently reducing our GDP by almost 2% (and the U.S. GDP only grew 1.7% in 2011).

The U.S. has not officially labeled China as a currency manipulator and has not fought back against China's trade war tactics primarily because of lobbying by U.S. multi-national corporations who are profiting by these activities.

The only way for U.S. corporations to access the world's second biggest and rapidly growing Chinese economy is to manufacture a large percentage of their product there, form partnerships and transfer technologies. These U.S. multi-national corporations fear that if the U.S. challenges China on their trading abuses that China will retaliate against the U.S. multi-nationals by further limiting their access to China's protected markets.

Once the U.S. manufacturers have established bases (invested capital) in China they want to be able to sell the goods they produce in China back to the U.S. as well and take advantage of the currency manipulation, lack of environmental regulations and exploitive labor practices; and replace their artificially higher cost facilities in the U.S.

This further drives down wages in the U.S. and has had a major impact in reducing our average real income to lower than it was in 1998. Not only is China's trade practices distorting the U.S. and Chinese markets, they are also stealing what should be our exports to other countries by creating an artificial currency advantage; and U.S. multi-nationals are also taking advantage of this position in trading to other countries through China.

In labor-intensive, low-skill industries, China would still hold a competitive advantage. However, these are the types of low paying jobs that we do not want for U.S. citizens and we should be appreciative that we can purchase these types of goods from our developing country trading partners. And these developing countries should be just as happy to be able to sell them to us.

However, the distortions created by China are so egregious that high value products in industries where the U.S. should be competitive (and that would provide attractive compensation for U.S. workers) are being artificially depressed to the extent that they are more cost effective to produce in China. The system is forcing the transfer of technologies to China, which will enable them to compete in ever higher value industries, which will further erode our future ability to compete based on technological capability and manufacturing know-how advantages.

As Chinese growth exploded in the 2000s, our trade deficit with them more than doubled between 2001 and 2008. During this time, the temporary boom in housing absorbed much of the labor of these lost jobs and it is only since the Great Recession that the true level of embezzlement allowed by our politicians has become apparent.

Fear mongering politicians argue that if we take action against China they will not purchase our debt and the U.S. economy will collapse. This is completely backwards thinking, we have to deficit spend in the U.S. because of the trade deficit with China that is reducing our income (stealing our jobs). In addition, since China is not spending those dollars they will have to end up as savings and enter into the Treasury market.

Politicians also incite fear that engaging in protectivism will spark a global trade war and worsen the economic condition by pointing to the effects of the Smoot-Hawley Tariff Act of 1933, which increased the severity of the Great Depression. However, China has been waging a trade war on the U.S. for 20 years with a significant impact on our economic viability through the loss of industries, jobs, income, and the reverse of savings (indebtedness).

We cannot allow China to continue its insidious trade practices. It must be acknowledged that China is not a trading partner but a trading enemy. The real war in which our country should be engaged, deploying all of the resources we can bring to bear with absolute resolution, is that against China's trade manipulation to regain our economic security.

It is not military prowess, but, access to our market, the largest, most diverse, and resilient economy in the world, that is the greatest weapon in the U.S. arsenal. China has been waging an economic war on the U.S. for more than 20 years and we have the right to defend our prosperity. It is the U.S. multi-national corporations and U.S. politicians that are the true enablers and co-conspirators of this plunder of U.S. economic resources.

Chapter Six

Battle of the Wonks

Death by Silver Bullet

Living is easy with eyes closed misunderstanding all you see,
It's getting hard to be someone but it all works out,
It doesn't matter much to me.
Let me take you down 'cause I'm going to Strawberry Fields,
Nothing is real and nothing to get hung about,
Strawberry Fields forever.
No one I think is in my tree I mean it must be high or low,
That is you can't you know tune in but it's all right,
That is I think it's not too bad.
Let me take you down 'cause I'm going to Strawberry Fields,
Nothing is real and nothing to get hung about,
Strawberry Fields forever.
Always, no sometime think it's me,
But you know I know when it's a dream,
I think -er no, I mean -er yes, but it's all wrong,
That is I think I disagree.

"Strawberry Fields Forever" – The Beatles

In the 1920s, Irving Fisher became the first American economist to reach celebrity status, though it was a brief stint. As just days before the Wall Street Crash of 1929 he proclaimed that "stock prices have reached what looks like a permanently high plateau," and the market was "only shaking out the lunatic fringe" as prices were not inflated and would go much higher. Fisher's prognostications not only cost him his personal wealth but his academic reputation. His misdiagnosis forced him to evaluate why he missed seeing the coming of the market crash which precipitated the Great Depression and he developed the Debt Deflation Theory of Great Depressions, in which he postulates that once you irrationally over-leverage with debt there are no silver bullets for dealing with the problem - no magical policy responses - only a slow and painful deleveraging process, and therefore, the key is the prevention of the irrational accumulation of debt.

Ben Bernanke is considered to be one of world's foremost economists on the subject of deflation. In 2000, Bernanke released his "Essays on the Great Depression," in which he dismissed Fisher's conclusion, stating, "it seems that the best research strategy is to push the rationality postulate as far as it will go."

Unfortunately, people are irrational actors. What may seem rational to an individual can be irrational when performed by the entire population. The Roaring Twenties had been a period of speculative booms and extremely irrational behavior in which small investors were purchasing on margin more than two-thirds the face value of their stock holdings and had borrowed more than the entire amount of currency in circulation. These actions led to a stock bubble in which prices increased fivefold and created the perception that stock prices would rise indefinitely.

In 2002 Bernanke gave a speech titled "Deflation: Making Sure 'It' Doesn't Happen Here," in which he states:

"The Congress has given the Fed the responsibility of preserving price stability (among other objectives), which most definitely implies avoiding deflation as well as inflation. I am confident that the Fed would take whatever means necessary to prevent significant deflation in the United States and, moreover, that the U.S. central bank, in cooperation with other parts of the government as needed, has sufficient policy instruments to ensure that any deflation that might occur would be both mild and brief. . . . As I have mentioned, some observers have concluded that when the central bank's policy rate falls to zero -- its practical minimum -- monetary policy loses its ability to further stimulate aggregate demand and the economy. At a broad conceptual level, and in my view in practice as well, this conclusion is clearly mistaken. Indeed, under a fiat (that is, paper) money system, a government (in practice, the central bank in cooperation with other agencies) should always be able to generate increased nominal spending and inflation, even when the short-term nominal interest rate is at zero."

He then prescribed seven actions the Federal Reserve could use to prevent deflation, which basically became his playbook for the Great Recession:

1. Increase the money supply. ". . . the U.S. government has a technology, called a printing press (or, today, its electronic equivalent), that allows it to produce as many U.S. dollars as it wishes at essentially no cost."
2. Ensure liquidity in financial markets.
3. Lower interest rates to their zero bound and then start to reduce longer-term interest rates through purchasing longer-maturity treasuries.
4. Facilitate lending to banks to encourage low yields on corporate bonds and other privately issued securities.
5. Depreciate the U.S. dollar.
6. Purchase foreign currencies to further depreciate the U.S. dollar.
7. Take equity stakes in banks and financial institutions (or support the U.S. government in doing so by monetizing the debt).

In this speech Bernanke also addressed the deflation being experienced in Japan (which had developed equity and real estate asset bubbles that popped in 1989):

"The claim that deflation can be ended by sufficiently strong action has no doubt led you to wonder, if that is the case, why has Japan not ended its deflation? . . . I believe that, when all is said and done, the failure to end deflation in Japan does not necessarily reflect any technical infeasibility of achieving that goal. Rather, it is a byproduct of a longstanding political debate about how best to address Japan's overall economic problems. . . . Japan's deflation problem is real and serious; but, in my view, political constraints, rather than a lack of policy instruments, explain why its deflation has persisted for as long as it has. Thus, I do not view the Japanese experience as evidence against the general conclusion that U.S. policymakers have the tools they need to prevent, and, if necessary, to cure a deflationary recession in the United States."

Three years prior to this speech, in 1999, Bernanke released a paper titled "Japanese Monetary Policy: A Case of Self-Induced Paralysis?" Within the paper he repeatedly asserts that Japan's low inflation (or deflation) was caused by inadequate aggregate demand and could be resolved by their central bank, stating:

". . . the slow or even negative rate of price increase points strongly to a diagnosis of aggregate demand deficiency. Note that if Japan's slow growth were due entirely to structural problems on the supply side, inflation rather than deflation would probably be in evidence."

In his study of the Great Depression, Bernanke recognized that significant errors were made in monetary policy responses that aggravated the situation, and he believed that if only the proper treatment had been provided the deflation would have been cured. He concludes that it is deflation itself that is the true danger as it would cause people's existing debts to become more onerous:

"The modern economy makes heavier use of credit, especially longer-term credit, than the economies of the nineteenth century. Further, unlike the earlier period, rising prices are the norm and are reflected in nominal-interest-rate setting to a much greater degree. . . . the evidence favors the view that deflation or even zero inflation is far more dangerous today than it was a hundred years ago."

He pays no homage to Fisher's conclusion that over-indebtedness must be prevented as all economic rules break down once you reach that state. Bernanke instead focuses on the central bank's ability to eradicate his perceived enemy - deflation:

". . . liquidity trap or no, monetary policy retains considerable power to expand nominal aggregate demand."

He is completely unaware that these are merely chronic and untreatable symptoms of debt deflation as described by Fisher.

Bernanke then reveals his lack of understanding of the disastrous effects of asset bubbles:

". . . . based on my earlier observation that money issuance must affect prices, else printing money will create infinite purchasing power. Suppose the Bank of Japan prints yen and uses them to acquire foreign assets. If the yen did not depreciate as a result, and if there were no reciprocal demand for Japanese goods or assets (which would drive up domestic prices), what in principle would prevent the BOJ from acquiring infinite quantities of foreign assets, leaving foreigners nothing to hold but idle yen balances? . . . there seems little reason not to try this strategy. The 'worst' that could happen would be that the BOJ would greatly increase its holdings of reserve assets."

Bernanke thought the "worst" that could happen by flaming speculation in assets was for the central bank to increase its holding of reserves. There is no appreciation for the role asset bubbles play in creating malinvestment, creating covert inflation, increasing speculation and perpetuating the debt accumulation which led to the deflationary environment.

Bernanke goes on to discuss how the Federal Reserve can monetize the debt so that the government does not have to issue treasuries to pay for its spending, making his now infamous helicopter reference:

"An alternate strategy, . . . is money-financed transfers to domestic households - - the real-life hoary thought experiment, the 'helicopter drop' of newly printed money. I think most economists would agree that a large enough helicopter drop must raise the price level. Suppose it did not, so that the price level remained unchanged. Then the real wealth of the population would grow without bound, as they are flooded with gifts of money from the government. . . . Surely at some point the public would attempt to convert its increased real wealth into goods and services, spending that would increase aggregate demand and prices. Conversion of the public's money wealth into other assets would also be beneficial, if it raised the prices of other assets."

Again, Bernanke is obsessed with averting deflation (creating inflation) and increasing aggregate demand with no appreciation for the disastrous impact of blowing asset bubbles.

Professor Bernanke then makes a statement that implicates the future Federal Reserve Chairman Bernanke of operating outside of the Federal Reserve's charter in bailing out the banks at the expense of the U.S. taxpayer:

"In thinking about nonstandard open-market operations, it is useful to separate those that have some fiscal component from those that do not. By a fiscal component I mean some implicit subsidy, such as would arise if the BOJ purchased nonperforming bank loans at face value, for example (this is of course equivalent to a fiscal bailout of the banks, financed by the central bank). This sort of money-financed 'gift' to the private sector would expand aggregate demand for the same reasons that any money-financed transfer does. . . . Nonstandard open-market operations with a fiscal component, even if legal, would be correctly viewed as an end run around the authority of the legislature, and so are better left in the realm of theoretical curiosities."

Finally, Bernanke touts the abilities of the establishment to be able to creatively address any economic scenario with little thought of the unintended consequences nor to the moral hazard created in even stating these views, never mind enacting them.

"Japanese monetary policy seems paralyzed, with a paralysis that is largely self-induced. Most striking is the apparent unwillingness of the monetary authorities to experiment, to try anything that isn't absolutely guaranteed to work."

Fisher warned of the paralyzing effects excessive debt had on monetary policy, and Bernanke has now been at the helm of the printing press long enough to understand that Japan's ineffectiveness in resolving their debt deflation problems were not self-induced as prevention is the only option.

I expect Bernanke has also come to accept that humans are irrational actors, that there are unpredictable and damaging effects of asset bubbles, and there is no such thing as an "aggregate" upon which you can base your assumptions.

Bernanke must also have gained an appreciation for the damage that can be inflicted by creative financing and the dangerous amplification mechanisms provided by our fractional reserve fiat monetary system (Fisher advocated for real money and no fractional reserve lending to provide greater protection from the inappropriate use of debt).

I believe what must be most shocking to Bernanke, is that he has learned that you cannot inflate your way out of debt deflation as real wages will not be able to keep up and real GDP will decline (and the non-wealthy will be subjected to greater suffering through financial repression).

The following chart shows Average Real Income from 1983-2010 in 2010 Dollars (Piketty-Saez):

Average Real Income in 2010 Dollars

Average real income is now below that of 1998, though since then, we have increased the total debt (public and private) by more than 100% of GDP.

Unfortunately, Bernanke was wrong and Fisher was right, there are no silver bullets that can resolve a debt deflation cycle; the typical monetary tools are rendered ineffective and we must now accept the consequences of having mortgaged our future "aggregate demand."

Bernanke has propped up equity markets by pumping money into the system through qualitative easing. This mainly benefits the wealthy, who are the majority shareholders, and to the extent that these dollars increase commodity speculation it hurts the non-wealthy who spend a much higher percent of their income on food, gas and other staples. Bernanke was hoping that by creating a wealth effect through inflating asset prices he would be able to increase aggregate demand, but, it is the wealthy (who are savers) that are benefiting while the non-wealthy are experiencing a decrease in real income through commodity inflation, therefore, it is net negative.

Bernanke has also focused on keeping the housing market from further deflating by purchasing mortgage securities and lowering the long-term interest rates by purchasing longer maturity treasuries. He hopes that lower long-term rates will also reach even further into the future to create aggregate demand today.

In reality, the only way aggregate demand has been increased (or maintained) is by the government becoming the borrower and spender of last resort with the Federal Reserve as co-conspirator in ensuring they can borrow endlessly at low rates. The Bush Tax Cuts were extended from which the wealthy are accruing significantly greater benefit than the middle class (tax cuts reduce government revenue and are equivalent to the government deficit spending).

Below is a chart that shows the government net spending (deficit) since 1990 in inflation adjusted 2005 dollars:

Federal Net Spending in 2005 $s

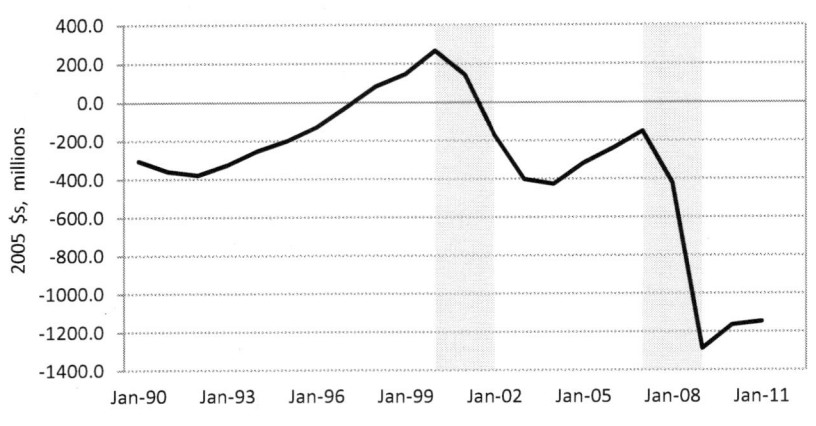

Source: U.S. Department of Commerce: Bureau of Economic Analysis/FRED

The official stimulus of the American Recovery and Reinvestment act of 2009 was estimated at the time to be $787 billion dollars and has since been upward revised to $831 billion. However, the unofficial stimulus continues through deficit spending.

And as the government grows, the distortions are increasing and the wealth gap is accelerating at a faster pace. The wealthy are receiving even greater benefits through their normal proprietary channels, while the non-wealthy are receiving their diminutive portion of government spending through safety net programs, and the dearth of the middle class continues.

As of January 2012, there are 46.5 million Americans on Food Stamps (a $82 billion per year program) comprising 20% of households. Since December 2007 there has been a 22% increase in workers receiving Social Security Disability Insurance .

The chart below shows Real Disposable Income and Real Disposable Income with the transfer payments of the safety net programs removed (in 2005 $s) from 2000 to 2012:

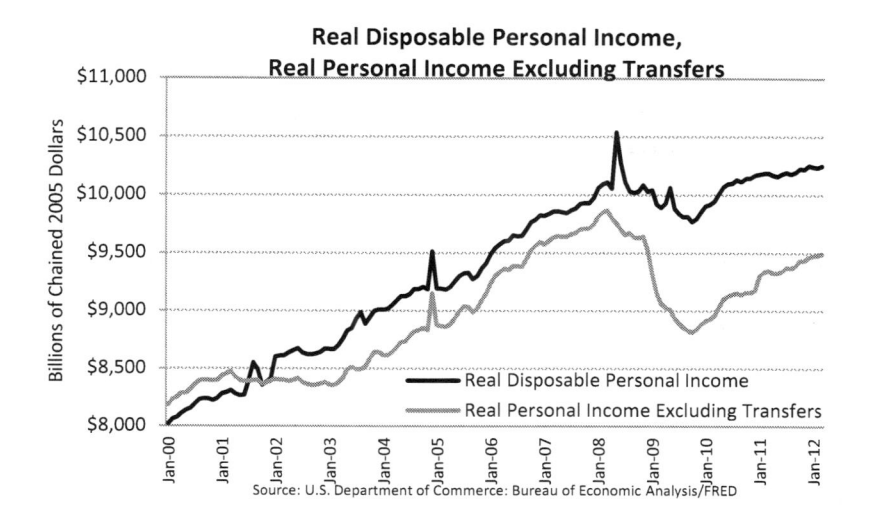

Real Disposable Personal Income, Real Personal Income Excluding Transfers

Source: U.S. Department of Commerce: Bureau of Economic Analysis/FRED

Bernanke's responses are continuing to increase the severity of the grossly inappropriate distribution of income and wealth in America. And as the wealthy are increasing their wealth, they are continuing to save and use their savings to create income. While the non-wealthy are falling further behind and are unable to take on the level of debt needed to match the quantity of savings the wealthy are creating.

Through his study of the Great Depression, Bernanke believed that modern economic theory and monetary tools could resolve any deflationary situation and had no appreciation that excessive debt would render all policy responses ineffective.

Bernanke's focus on aggregate demand caused him to overlook the bipolar distribution of income that is increasing savings for the wealthy (reducing aggregate demand) while reducing real income of the non-wealthy (also reducing aggregate demand).

Bernanke believed inflation could be used as a tool to reduce debt burdens and create demand led growth, however, he now realizes that the real income of the non-wealthy is not keeping up with inflation and therefore real growth cannot be created.

Bernanke engaged in quantitative easing and reduced long-term interest rates to increase asset values (pulling forward future gains) with the hope of increasing aggregate demand. However, it is the wealthy who own the assets that have benefited from the increase in asset values and they are saving their income and redistributing their investments into riskier assets in search of higher yields while creating greater misappropriations of capital through malinvestment. Furthermore, this speculation is stoking commodity price inflation, which is increasing the financial repression of the non-wealthy who continue to experience a decrease in their real incomes, and those who are on fixed incomes are being devastated by the low-interest rate environment.

The crux of the policy response continues to be dependent upon government deficit spending to allow the wealthy to save and to provide a safety net for the non-wealthy. This is further increasing the core problem of chronic income inequality that displays symptoms of decreasing aggregate demand and increasing indebtedness.

Chapter Seven

Disinheritance

Outside the street's on fire,
In a real death waltz,
Between what's flesh and what's fantasy.
And the poets down here,
Don't write nothing at all,
They just stand back and let it all be.
And in the quick of the night,
They reach for their moment,
And try to make an honest stand.
But they wind up wounded,
Not even dead.
Tonight in Jungleland.

Jungleland – Bruce Springsteen

We leave to the next generation the economy's ability to allow people to earn income and be able to obtain goods and services as well as passing on the governmental productivity impacts of distortions, incentives and distributions which will ultimately determine their standard of living.

The deregulation of the banking industry and the creation of shadow banking institutions has greatly distorted our economy towards financial engineering, which does not create real goods and services but seeks to leverage privileged access to money to create outsized returns for the elite.

Financial engineering facilitated debt creation through new vehicles that disguised risk and pulled forward demand while amplifying returns. These actions have accelerated the transfer of income from the productive citizens to the wealthy asset owners. This concentration of wealth to the few is increasing their ability to influence government, which is causing even greater distortions.

Moreover, government itself is growing. The chart below shows the spending of local, state and federal governments since 1901 as a percentage of GDP (negative areas show transfers from the federal government):

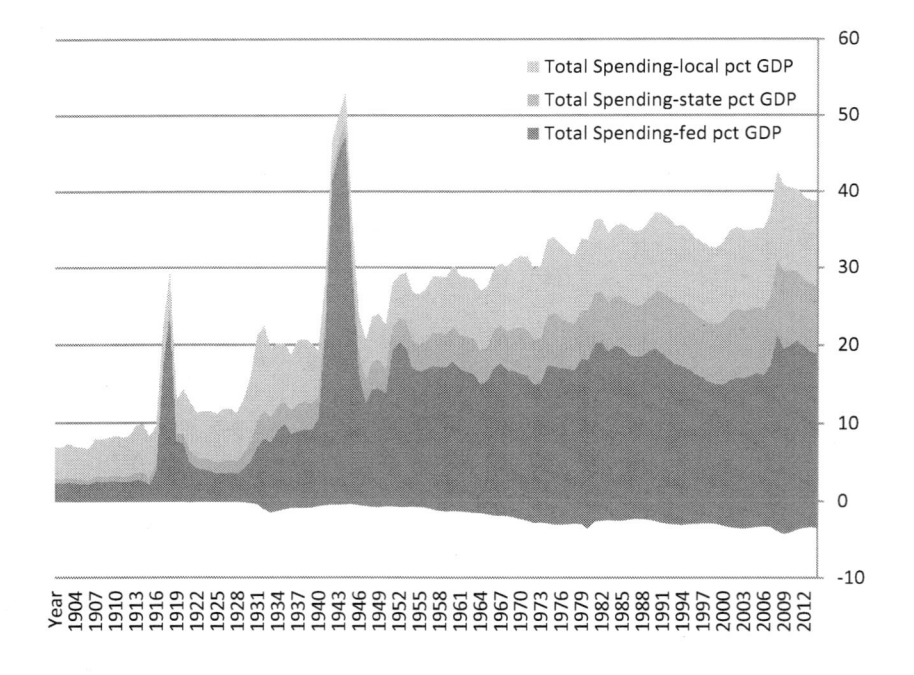

Government now spends forty cents of every dollar in our economy and not only has the growth of the government increased distortions, but, the government in itself is extremely inefficient as it has no competition.

As government has grown, so has the financial repression on the productive members of our society. Our economy is transforming into an ever more segregated society with a rapidly shrinking middle class. Following this path, we will continue to create a larger percentage of citizens dependent on safety net programs from an ever bigger government that is influenced by the concentrated wealth of the few while our commerce becomes directed toward creating luxury goods and services for the wealthy. As the distortions increase there will be higher levels of malinvestment and less incentive to engage in productivity activity.

We must eliminate all government we possibly can and transfer all remaining activities to the lowest level possible where the local communities will have the greatest influence on the best use of its resources.

As the currency issuer, the federal government poses the greatest danger. There is tremendous moral hazard for any activity at this level as they have an accomplice in the Federal Reserve who through treasury monetization have allowed Washington DC to shirk all fiscal responsibilities and create endless budget deficits. This by far is the most egregious action of the Federal Reserve; permitting fiscal recklessness through supportive monetary policies that have allowed the government to grow beyond what the free markets would have borne.

We must stop looking to government to solve our problems and recognize that it is the very policies of government and government itself that distorts markets and are creating the inefficiencies that are causing us to lose our global competitiveness.

We never should have ended up in such a perverse situation. However, the policy response to our economic crisis has been counterproductive by further increasing our debt, pulling in future demand and creating bigger government. The more appropriate response would have been to invest in infrastructure projects that were finite in time, would not increase the size of government and would result in a productivity gain or a reduction in future costs. And though infrastructure projects would be far more effective than the covert stimulus we have today (through running a deficit), we should not trust government to be able to accomplish any activity efficiently and I am quite uncomfortable offering this as a solution (as we have built far too many bridges-to-nowhere). The only way I would support such a proposal is if it was offered in support of a parallel plan that reduced the size of government while these projects provided an economic transition.

We are currently experiencing only modest growth even with huge government deficits because not only are we trapped in what Fisher deemed as debt deflation but because all business people understand that the economy is being artificially propped up by government spending. Therefore, they will not invest in new capital or hire new employees as they do not believe there is sustainable growth. Multi-national companies, which are experiencing record high profit margins (because of low-interest costs, wage deflation and government spending), are investing their profits in developing countries where they are forecasting strong growth.

The only way to eliminate government's current role as borrower and spender of last resort is to commit to a long-term plan to reduce government itself; of which people will be cognizant that this will increase productivity and allow real economic growth.

Many economists are screaming that the high unemployment is creating lost productivity and degrading workers' skills. Therefore, the government should be borrowing and spending even more. These economists have little appreciation for the long-term effects of creating bigger government and aggravating the root cause problems of crony capitalism which have resulted in massive income distribution issues while increasing inefficiencies and distortions.

Neither the government nor the wealthy are job creators. Just as the non-wealthy are capable of borrowing the wealthy's excess savings to deficit spend, so are the non-wealthy entrepreneurs capable of borrowing the wealthy's excess savings to create real jobs. Moreover, it is the wealthy's excess savings that is creating the aggregate demand problem. And the government is deficit spending by borrowing the excess savings of the wealthy to allow the wealthy to save their income (which was earned primarily through the investment of money versus productive activity).

Aggregate demand and excess savings are merely symptoms. The root problem is a crony capitalism induced distortion of income distribution; with the non-wealthy no longer capable of taking on the additional debt to make up for the excess income that the wealthy desire to save.

In 2011, to achieve 1.7% GDP growth the government deficit spent 8.6% of GDP or $1.3 trillion. Of this $1.3 trillion, $579 billion was saved by wealthy foreigners (the trade deficit) and the remaining $721 billion was saved by wealthy Americans (this includes corporations as well as individuals). The chart below depicting Total Consumer Credit

Outstanding since 1990 demonstrates that the non-wealthy (who are the users of consumer credit) have not yet been able to save and pay down their debt:

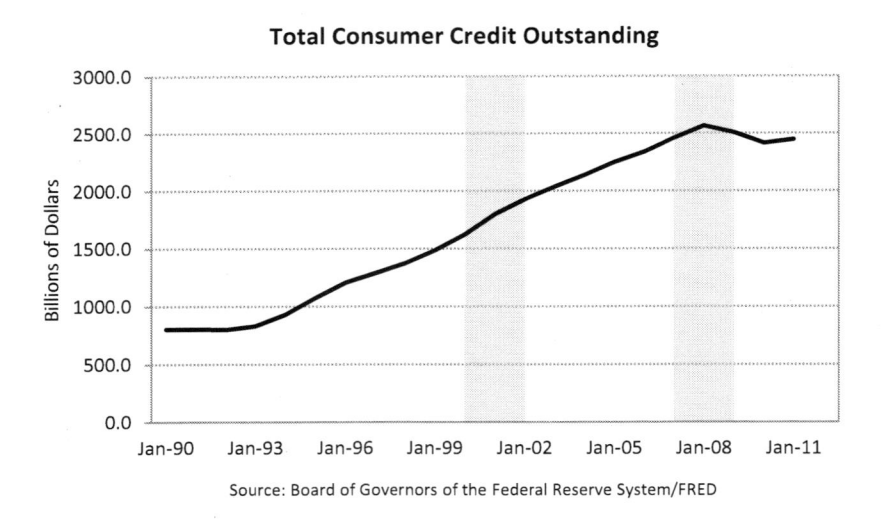

Total Consumer Credit Outstanding

Source: Board of Governors of the Federal Reserve System/FRED

Though I have attempted to provide fundamental economic principles that can be applied to evaluate any policy, there is one specific recommendation that I believe may be the most powerful lever we can pull in starting to address our core issues: a revenue neutral modification to our tax system that would eliminate all deductions (loopholes) to allow for a reduction in the marginal tax rate.

For every dollar that marginal taxes are reduced, GDP is increased by two to three dollars after about three years. The opposite is also true; for every dollar that marginal taxes are increased, GDP is decreased by two to three dollars after about three years. By eliminating deductions you would experience a reduction in the amount of economic activity that those distortions created; however, these loopholes are enjoyed by relatively few and the effects of lowering marginal taxes rates for the majority will have a far greater effect on increasing GDP (as well as creating less distorted and more efficient markets).

I would like to see the smallest government possible and the lowest level of taxation for all citizens. However, it is the wealthy's excess savings that are creating an aggregate demand problem and there is no reason that the wealthy should be paying lower tax rates than the middle class. In fact, this hurts the economy as the middle class is far more likely to spend their income and foster economic growth. I do not advocate redistribution of wealth through taxation. However, I hope that I have completely dispelled the myth that the wealthy should receive preferential tax treatment because they are job creators.

We are at a critical economic juncture and it is time to take an honest stand, expose the real problems, and change our path. Not only are we heading down the wrong track, we have not even begun to address the freight train heading towards us in the form of $59 trillion of unfunded liabilities for Social Security, Medicare and Medicaid.

Postscript

The Lights Are Off But Everybody's Home

The Silent Majority

Tyranny, like hell, is not easily conquered;
Yet we have this consolation with us,
That the harder the conflict,
The more glorious the triumph.
What we obtain too cheap,
We esteem too lightly;
'Tis dearness only that gives everything its value.
Heaven knows how to put a proper price upon its goods;
And it would be strange indeed,
If so celestial an article as freedom,
Should not be highly rated.

Thomas Paine, 1776

America's cynicism that the government has been corrupted beyond repair has never been higher. It is now believed to take more than three-quarters a billion dollars to run for president, $10 million to run for Senate and $5 million to run for Congress. The recognition that the money of special interest groups is controlling government by funding the campaigns of their puppets is making people focus more on how they can get their piece of the plunder than on how to rectify the perversions.

It is felt that even when people with good intentions get elected, they are instantly corrupted by the system once they get to Washington DC and realize that they better start playing by the rules of the establishment if they want to get reelected and preserve their own self-interests.

Enlightenment in America is now considered to be *wise enough to understand that there is nothing you can do to fix the system and it is the fool who expends precious energy on futile tasks.* There is a collective belief that Americans are not smart enough to understand that they are being manipulated by sound bites of misdirections, prayed on by fear mongering, and manipulated by emotional issues.

It is exactly this demoralization and sense of impotence that the establishment seeks to instill. This is what maintains their dominance and control.

But today, technology is changing the landscape. There has never been more access to credible information, or ability to communicate, and this means individuals are beginning to challenge the economic myths that have been previously accepted as doctrine. These tools can also be used to spread deception, but because of the many critical thinkers unwilling to yield to propaganda, I believe the tide has greatly shifted in the favor of truth.

There are 314 million Americans and only 435 congressmen, 100 senators, and 1 president. We can find in our communities those who we respect to lead, to fight, to speak the difficult truths, and to represent the majority without bowing to the minority special interest groups.

It will not be easy, but, we must restore America to the ideals our forefathers' intended and rekindle the dream for future generations. In the pursuit of happiness, all we ask for is a more even playing field.